S0-BCY-227

Taxes Made Simple:

Income Taxes
Explained in 100 Pages or Less

Taxes Made Simple:

Income Taxes
Explained in 100 Pages or Less

Mike Piper

Simple Subjects, LLC
Chicago, Illinois 60626
ISBN: 978-0-9814542-1-4
www.simplesubjects.com/tax

Dedication

For the lifelong student.

Table of Contents

Part Three
Important Deductions and Credits

Part Four
Other Important Things to Know

Introduction

Like the other books in the *"...in 100 Pages or Less"* series, this book is based on the assumptions that:

a) You're looking to gain a basic understanding of the book's topic (in this case, income taxes), and
b) You don't relish the thought of spending a great deal of time on the effort.

If that's not the case, and you *are* looking for something that's going to turn you into an expert on the topic of income taxes, then you've got the wrong book. Save yourself some time, and go look for a different book. This isn't the one for you.

Why Bother Learning This Stuff?

You wouldn't be holding this book unless you had a sense of the importance of having at least a ground-level understanding of taxation, but I do want to touch briefly upon one point.

What many people misunderstand about taxation is the fact that (even if they don't prepare their own tax returns every year) a little bit of tax knowledge can be quite valuable. The reason, of

7

course, is that by the time your accountant is preparing your tax return, it's frequently too late to do any of the things that you could have done over the course of the year to reduce your tax burden.

The Goal

Ideally, by the time you're finished reading:

- You'll be familiar with income tax terminology.
- You'll understand how all the variables interact to determine how much you get back or owe come next tax season.
- You'll be aware of a few strategies to help reduce your taxes.
- And maybe (depending upon your interest level and the complexity of your return), you'll find that you're capable of preparing your own tax return next season.

How We're Going to Get You There

This book is broken down into four parts:

1. A quick run-through of the basics (such as the differences between deductions and credits).

2. A look at the different types of taxable income and gains, and how each is taxed.
3. An explanation of several important deductions and credits that could help you reduce your taxes, and
4. An overview of a handful of other topics such as state taxes and the Alternative Minimum Tax.

So without further ado...

PART ONE

The Basics

CHAPTER ONE

Income Tax: It's Progressive!

The Federal income tax is referred to as a "progressive tax." Of course, it's not progressive in the same way that a social movement could be said to be progressive. What the term means in this case is that, as your taxable income increases, so does the rate at which you are taxed.

People will often make statements such as "I'm in the 25% tax bracket." For example, as you can see on the next page, a single person with a taxable income of $40,000 would be in the 25% tax bracket.[1] People frequently misunderstand this to mean that all of the person's income is taxed at a rate of 25%. In reality, the person's overall tax rate will be much lower.

---

[1] Tax brackets, like many other parts of the tax code, change on a yearly basis in an effort to adjust for inflation.

11

Single (2009)

If taxable income is over:	But not over:	The tax is:
$0	$8,350	10% of the amount over $0
$8,350	$33,950	$835 plus 15% of the amount over $8,350
$33,950	$82,250	$4,675 plus 25% of the amount over $33,950
$82,250	$171,550	$16,750 plus 28% of the amount over $82,250
$171,550	$372,950	$41,754 plus 33% of the amount over $171,550
$372,950	no limit	$108,216 plus 35% of the amount over $372,950

EXAMPLE: Samantha's 2009 taxable income is $40,000. This puts her in the 25% tax bracket. If that meant that all of her income was taxed at 25%, she would be paying $10,000 in income taxes. Instead, she'll be paying much less. Samantha will actually end up paying $6,187.50 calculated as follows:

1) Her first $8,350 of taxable income is taxed at 10%. ($835 in tax)
2) From $8,350 to $33,950 she's taxed at 15%. ($3,840 in tax)
3) From $33,950 to $40,000 Sam is taxed at 25%. ($1,512.50 in tax)
4) $835 + $3,840 + $1,512.50 = $6,187.50

Filing Status

Your tax bracket depends upon two things: your taxable income and your filing status. The options for filing status are:

1. Single
2. Married Filing Jointly
3. Married Filing Separately
4. Head of Household
5. Qualifying Widower with Dependent Child (This can apply to widows as well as widowers.)

Your filing status is based upon your marital and family situation on the *last* day of the tax year. If on the last day of the tax year, multiple filing statuses apply to you, you are allowed to choose between them.

Single
(tax brackets on page 12)
For unmarried taxpayers.

Married Filing Jointly (2009)

If taxable income is over:	But not over:	The tax is:
$0	$16,700	10% of the amount over $0
$16,700	$67,900	$1,670 plus 15% of the amount over $16,700
$67,900	$137,050	$9,350 plus 25% of the amount over $67,900
$137,050	$208,850	$26,637.50 plus 28% of the amount over $137,050
$208,850	$372,950	$46,741.50 plus 33% of the amount over $208,850
$372,950	no limit	$100,894.50 plus 35% of the amount over $372,950

Married Filing Jointly

For married couples who file a joint return that includes all of their combined income and deductions.

Married Filing Separately (2009)

If taxable income is over:	But not over:	The tax is:
$0	$8,350	10% of the amount over $0
$8,350	$33,950	$835 plus 15% of the amount over $8,350
$33,950	$68,525	$4,675 plus 25% of the amount over $33,950
$68,525	$104,425	$13,318.75 plus 28% of the amount over $68,525
$104,425	$186,475	$23,370.75 plus 33% of the amount over $104,425
$186,475	no limit	$50,447.25 plus 35% of the amount over $186,475

Married Filing Separately

For married couples who file separate returns. For the most part, this isn't a beneficial thing to do. Generally, married couples who file separate returns are doing so because they are, in fact, separated (though still married), not because of any tax benefit to be gained.

15

Head of Household (2009)

If taxable income is over:	But not over:	The tax is:
$0	$11,950	10% of the amount over $0
$11,950	$45,500	$1,195 plus 15% of the amount over $11,950
$45,500	$117,450	$6,227.50 plus 25% of the amount over $45,500
$117,450	$190,200	$24,215 plus 28% of the amount over $117,450
$190,200	$372,950	$44,585.00 plus 33% of the amount over $190,200
$372,950	no limit	$104,892.50 plus 35% of the amount over $372,950

Head of Household

Unmarried taxpayers who support one or more dependents may be able to file as Head of Household. To qualify to file as Head of Household, you must:
- Be unmarried on the last day of the year,
- Pay more than half the cost of keeping up a home for the year, and
- Have had a "qualifying dependent[1]" live with you for more than half of the year.

---

[1] For more information about qualifying dependents, see Table 4 in Publication 501: http://www.irs.gov/publications/p501/

Qualifying Widower with Dependent Child

If you are eligible to file as a Qualifying Widower with Dependent Child, you can use the married filing jointly tax brackets and the married filing jointly standard deduction rate (explained in Chapter 3). To be eligible to file as a qualifying widower in 2009, you must meet all of the following requirements:

- You were eligible to file a joint return with your spouse in the year of his/her death.
- Your spouse died in 2009, 2008, or 2007 and you did not remarry before the end of 2009.
- You have a child or stepchild for whom you can claim an exemption.
- The child lived in your home all year.
- You paid more than half of the cost of keeping up the home over the course of the year.

What's a "Marginal Tax Bracket?"

Sometimes when reading about taxes, you'll come across the term "marginal tax bracket." While it sounds complicated, all the term really refers to is the highest tax bracket that your taxable income reaches. The significance of knowing your marginal tax bracket is explained best with an example.

EXAMPLE: Lauren is single, and her taxable income is $40,000. Therefore, her marginal tax bracket is 25%. This allows her to determine the real, after-tax value of an increase in her income.

Her employer offers her an $8,000 raise in exchange for accepting some additional responsibilities at work. Because Lauren's marginal tax rate is 25%, she knows she'll only get to keep 75% of the extra income. The after-tax value of the proposed raise is only $6,000.

Chapter 1 Simple Summary

- The Federal income tax is a progressive tax, meaning that the more you earn, the higher your tax rate.

- Due to this progressive structure, a person's income will be taxed (in total) at a lower rate than would seem to be indicated by the statement, "I'm in the ___% tax bracket."

- Your tax rate depends not just on your taxable income, but also on your filing status (single, married filing jointly, etc.).

- Your marginal tax bracket is simply the highest tax bracket that applies to you.

CHAPTER TWO

Where Tax Law Comes From

Even though it will neither help you prepare your taxes, nor save you money, this topic is important enough for a brief mention.

It's Not the IRS

Despite a public misunderstanding to the contrary, the Internal Revenue Service does not create the tax law in our country. Rather, *Congress* creates it (just like every other Federal law). The IRS is only responsible for *administering* the tax law.

So the next time you see or read about a Senator or Representative complaining about the "IRS's tax code" and how it's made taxes too high, too low, or too complicated (depending upon the speaker's political affiliation), don't buy it. If there's someone to blame, it's the lawmakers themselves—or we who voted for those lawmakers.

If you have an issue with a particular aspect of the tax code, don't sit there cursing the IRS. Take the issue up with your Senator (or, if you want a better chance of being listened to), your Representative. It is, after all, their *job* to represent their constituents.

OK. That's it. I'm off my soapbox. Let's move on.

Chapter 2 Simple Summary

- The IRS doesn't create the tax law. It only administers it. Congress creates tax law.

- If you think the tax code needs to be changed, don't just complain about it. Complain to the people who can do something about it.

CHAPTER THREE

Exemptions, Deductions, and Credits: What's the Difference?

Many taxpayers are confused as to the difference between exemptions, deductions, and credits. Essentially, the difference is that deductions and exemptions both reduce your taxable *income*, while credits reduce your *tax*.

Exemptions

Exemptions reduce your taxable income. They are the result of tax breaks granted by the government. For 2009, you are entitled to an exemption of $3,650 for yourself, one for your spouse, and one for each of your dependents.

21

EXAMPLE: Kevin and Jennifer are married, and they have three children, whom they claim as dependents. They will be allowed five exemptions. As a result, their taxable income will be reduced by $18,250.

Deductions

Deductions generally arise from your expenses. For example, a deduction is allowed for interest paid on student loans.

EXAMPLE: Carlos is in the 25% tax bracket. Over the course of the year, he paid $1,600 in student loan interest. This $1,600 decrease in his taxable income will save him $400 in taxes ($1,600 x 25%).

Itemized Deductions or Standard Deduction?

Several deductions (such as charitable contributions or the interest on your home mortgage) fall into the category known as "itemized" deductions. Sometimes, these are known as "below the line" deductions (more on that in the next section). Every year, you have the choice to use either:

1. The sum of all of your itemized deductions, or

2. The standard deduction ($5,700 for a single taxpayer in 2009, or $11,400 for a married couple filing jointly).

For the most part, this decision is pretty easy. Simply add up all of your itemized deductions[1], and compare the total to the standard deduction you would be allowed. Then simply take whichever option allows you a larger deduction.

Above the Line vs. Below the Line Deductions

If a deduction does not fall into the category of itemized, or "below the line," it must be what is known as an "above the line" deduction. Above the line deductions are unique in that you can claim them regardless of whether you choose to use the standard deduction or your itemized deductions.

Some common above the line deductions include contributions to a traditional IRA, interest paid on student loans, or contributions to a Health Savings Account.

In contrast to above the line deductions, which are always useful, below the line/itemized deductions are only valuable if and to the extent that

---

[1] We'll be discussing specific itemized deductions in later chapters, or you can see the instructions to Schedule A for more information: www.irs.gov/pub/irs-pdf/i1040sa.pdf

23

they (in total) exceed your standard deduction amount. Here's how it looks mathematically:

Gross Income (sum of all your sources of income)
— <u>Above the line deductions</u>
= Adjusted Gross Income ← "The Line"
— Standard Deduction *or* Itemized Deductions
— <u>Exemptions</u>
= Taxable Income

EXAMPLE: Eddie is a single taxpayer. During the year he contributes $3,000 to a traditional IRA, and he makes a charitable contribution of $1,000 to Kiva.org (his favorite non-profit). He has no other deductions, and his income (before deductions) is $50,000.

The IRA contribution is an above the line deduction, and the charitable donation is a below the line (a.k.a. itemized) deduction.

Plugging this into the above equation, we get this:

Gross Income	$50,000
—Above the line deductions	—$3,000
= Adjusted Gross Income	= $47,000
—Exemption	—$3,650
—Standard deduction	—$5,700
= Taxable Income	= $37,650

Important observations:

1. Eddie's itemized deductions ($1,000) are less in total than his standard deduction ($5,700). As such, Eddie's charitable contribution doesn't provide him with any tax benefit, because he'll elect to use his standard deduction instead of his itemized deductions.
2. Eddie's above the line deduction provides a tax benefit even though he's using the standard deduction.

Again, itemized/below the line deductions only help when they add up to an amount greater than your standard deduction. Above the line deductions, on the other hand, are *always* beneficial.

Credits

Unlike deductions and exemptions, credits reduce your taxes directly, dollar for dollar. After determining the total amount of tax you owe, you then subtract the dollar value of the credits for which you are eligible. This makes credits particularly valuable.

Credits arise from a number of things. Most often, though, they are the result of the taxpayer doing something that Congress has decided is beneficial for the community. For example, you are allowed a credit of up to $2,500 for paying "qualified

25

education expenses" for one of your dependents. If you meet the requirements[1] to claim the maximum credit, your *tax* (not taxable income) will be reduced by $2,500.

"Pre-Tax Money"

You'll often hear the term "pre-tax money," generally used in a context along the lines of "Hey, I just found out I can pay for [something] with pre-tax money!" This means one of two things:

1. The item is deductible, or
2. The item can be paid for automatically in the form of a deduction from your paycheck.[2]

The reason these situations are sometimes referred to as "pre-tax" is that you get to spend this money before the government takes their cut. This makes it more cost-effective for you.

You will, from time to time, run across people who seem to be under the impression that something is free simply because it's deductible or because they were allowed to spend pre-tax money on it. This is a severe misunderstanding. Being able to

---

[1] Discussed in detail in Chapter 10.
[2] Note: Some things that can be paid for with payroll deductions are not, in fact, tax deductible. A quick search on the IRS's website should help if you're unsure about any particular item.

26

spend pre-tax money on something is much more akin to getting a discount on it than it is to getting the item free.

Chapter 3 Simple Summary

- You are entitled to one exemption for yourself, one for your spouse, and one for each of your dependents. In 2009, each exemption reduces your taxable income by $3,650.

- Deductions arise from your expenses, and they reduce your taxable income.

- Each year, you can use *either* your standard deduction *or* the sum of all your itemized (below the line) deductions.

- Above the line deductions are particularly valuable because you can use them regardless of whether you use your standard deduction or itemized deductions.

- Credits, unlike deductions and exemptions, reduce your tax directly (as opposed to reducing your taxable income). Therefore, a credit is always more valuable than a deduction of the same amount.

27

CHAPTER FOUR

Calculating Your Refund
(or Lack Thereof)

Many taxpayers in the U.S. have come to expect a nice treat every year in the form of a tax refund. To some people who don't prepare their own tax returns, it's a mystery how the refund is calculated.

The idea is really quite simple. After calculating your taxable income, you use the information in the tax tables (page 12-16) to determine your total income tax for the year. This amount is then compared to the amount that you actually paid throughout the year (in the form of withholdings from your paychecks). If the amount you paid is *more* than your tax, you are entitled to a refund for the difference. On the other hand, if the amount you paid is *less* than your tax, it's time to get out the checkbook.

Withholding: Why It's Done

If you work as an employee, you're certainly aware that a large portion of your wages/salary doesn't actually show up in your paycheck every two weeks. Instead, it gets "withheld."

The reason for this is that the Federal government wants to be absolutely sure that it gets its money. The government knows that many people have a tendency to spend literally all of the income they receive (if not more). As a result, the government set up the system so that it would get its share before taxpayers would have a chance to spend it.

The amount of your pay that gets withheld is based upon an estimate of how much tax you'll be responsible for paying over the course of the year. Your employer's calculations for withholding are based upon what they expect your income to be, and how many exemptions you will be claiming. (This is why people are required to fill out Form W-4 indicating how many dependents they have when they start a new job.)

Withholding: How It's Calculated

At this point you may be thinking, "OK. Well I just learned that I'm in the ___% tax bracket, and it's obvious that my employer is withholding *way* more than that!"

29

You're probably right. That's because your employer isn't just withholding for Federal income taxes. They're also withholding for social security taxes, Medicare taxes, and (likely) state income taxes.

Social security taxes are calculated as 6.2% of your earnings, and Medicare taxes are calculated as 1.45% of your earnings. Before you've even begun to pay your income taxes, 7.65% of your income has been withheld.

Great. So...How Much Is My Refund?

Your refund is calculated by comparing your total income tax (based upon the tax brackets on pages 12-16) to the amount that was withheld for Federal income tax. Assuming that the amount withheld for Federal income tax was greater than your income tax for the year, the difference is the refund that you'll receive.

EXAMPLE: Nick's total taxable income (after subtracting deductions and exemptions) is $35,000. He is single. Using the table on page 12, we can determine that his Federal income tax is $4,937.50.

Over the course of the year, Nick's employer withheld a total of $9,000 from his pay, but only $6,000 of that was to go toward Federal income tax. His refund will be $1,062.50. ($6,000 − $4,937.50)

30

Chapter 4 Simple Summary

- Every year, your refund is calculated as the amount *withheld* for Federal income tax, minus your total Federal income tax for the year (calculated using tables on pages 12-16).

- A large portion of the money being withheld from each of your paychecks does not actually go toward Federal income tax. Instead, it goes to pay social security and Medicare taxes (and possibly state income taxes).

PART TWO

Taxable Income & Taxable Gains

CHAPTER FIVE

Taxable Income

It's obvious that, in addition to your filing status, the size of your taxable income is the most important factor in how much tax you'll be responsible for paying every year. What's not so obvious is that the calculation of your tax is also affected by the *type(s)* of income that you earn.

There are four primary categories of income:

1. Salaries and Wages
2. Earnings from Self-Employment
3. Interest Income
4. Dividend Income

Salaries and Wages

For most people, the majority of income comes in the form of salaries and wages. Salaries and wages are straightforward in terms of taxes because they are taxable at the normal tax rates (pages 12-16), and they are subject to normal social security and Medicare taxes (explained on page 30).

If you work as an employee, your salary or wages for each year will be reported to you on Form W-2 at the beginning of the following year. The amount withheld for Federal income tax, state income taxes, and social security and Medicare taxes is also reported on your W-2.

Earnings from Self-Employment

Earnings from self-employment are subject to the same income tax rates as wages or salaries. However, instead of being subject to social security and Medicare taxes, self-employment earnings are subject to the Self-Employment Tax.

For employees of a company, a social security tax of 6.2% and Medicare tax of 1.45% are withheld from each paycheck. The person's employer is required to pay a matching amount. So the employee is paying 7.65%, and the employer is paying 7.65% for a grand total of 15.3%. When you're self-employed, you are, in essence, both the employee

34

and the employer, so you get stuck with both halves of the bill (15.3%).

In contrast to people who work as employees (who get their income reported to them on a W-2), business owners are responsible for keeping records of how much their businesses make over the course of the year. If, however, you work as an independent contractor, your income—as long as it's over $600—will be reported to you on Form 1099. (If it's under $600, it won't be reported to you on any form at all, though you're still responsible for reporting it on your tax return.)

Interest Income

Most interest income—such as that from a savings account—is subject to normal income tax rates (like salaries, wages, and self-employment income). However, one advantage of interest income is that it is not subject to social security and Medicare taxes. Taxable interest income that you earn will be reported to you on Form 1099-INT.

Some types of interest income are unique in that they are not subject to Federal taxation at all. This category of income is, understandably, referred to as nontaxable interest income. The two most common sources of nontaxable interest income are bonds issued by state governments and bonds issued by municipalities. One important thing to know is

35

that, while it's not subject to Federal taxation, nontaxable interest income will often be subject to state or local income taxes.

Dividend Income

Dividends—distributions of a corporation's profits to the shareholders—are also taxable. Like interest income, dividend income is not subject to social security or Medicare taxes.

Also, dividend income may be subject to lower income tax rates than other types of income. If a dividend meets a list of requirements, it will be referred to as a "qualified dividend." Qualified dividends are subject to a maximum tax rate of 15%. Generally, dividends that you receive for shares of stock that you've held for at least the last 60 days will be qualified dividends.

Because your Form 1099-DIV (received from your brokerage firm) will indicate what portion of your dividends were qualified dividends, it generally isn't necessary to concern yourself with memorizing all the specific requirements for a dividend to be a qualified dividend.[1]

---

[1] If, however, you are interested, the requirements are explained in IRS Publication 550, available at
http://www.irs.gov/publications/p550/

Chapter 5 Simple Summary

Type of Income	Income Tax Rate	Subject to Social Security and Medicare?
Wages/Salary	Normal rates	Yes
Self-Employment Income	Normal rates	Subject to Self-Employment Tax instead
Interest Income	Normal rates	No
Dividend Income	Max of 15%	No

CHAPTER SIX

Capital Gains and Losses

When you sell something (such as a share of stock) for more than you paid for it, you're generally going to be taxed on the increase in value. This increase in value is known as a "capital gain."

The amount of gain is calculated as the proceeds received from the sale, minus your "adjusted cost basis."

What on Earth Does "Adjusted Cost Basis" Mean?

In most cases, your adjusted cost basis in an asset is simply the amount that you paid for that asset.[1]

---

[1] If you did not actually *buy* the asset (i.e., gifts, inheritances, etc.) your cost basis will depend upon other factors, explained in Publication 551, available at:
http://www.irs.gov/publications/p551/

(Note: This includes any brokerage fees that you paid on the transaction.)

EXAMPLE: Lauren buys a share of Google® stock for $250, including brokerage fees. She owns it for two years and then sells it for $400. Her adjusted cost basis is the amount she paid for it: $250. Her gain will be calculated as follows:

$400 (proceeds from sale)
- $250 (adjusted cost basis)
= $150 (capital gain)

Long Term Capital Gains vs. Short Term Capital Gains

The rate of tax charged on a capital gain depends upon whether it was a long term capital gain (LTCG) or a short term capital gain (STCG). If the asset in question was held for one year or less, it's a short term capital gain. If the asset was held for greater than one year, it's a long term capital gain.

STCGs are taxed at normal income tax rates. LTCGs, however, are taxed at a maximum of 15%. So if you're ever considering selling an investment that's increased in value, it might be a good idea to think about holding the asset long enough for the capital gain to be considered long term.

Note that a capital gain occurs only when the asset is sold. This is important because it means that fluctuations in the value of the asset don't constitute a taxable event.

EXAMPLE: Beth buys ten shares of Honda Motor Company® at $25 each. Five years later, Beth still owns the shares, and the price per share has risen to $45. Over the five years, Beth isn't required to pay any tax on the increase in value. She will only have to pay a tax on the LTCG if/when she chooses to sell the shares.

Why Taxation of Mutual Funds Is So Very Strange

Mutual funds are taxed in a way that sets them apart from other investments.

Drastically simplified version:
In essence, mutual funds shareholders are taxed every year based upon the changes in the values of the funds that they own. Note how this is unlike other investments, which are taxed only when the asset is sold.

More precise (longer) version:
Mutual funds are collections of a very large quantity of other investments. For instance, a mutual fund

40

may own thousands of different stocks as well as any number of other investments like bonds or CDs.

Each year, a mutual fund (like any other investor) is responsible for paying taxes on the net capital gains it incurred over the course of the year. However, instead of the mutual fund paying those taxes itself, each of the fund's shareholders pays taxes on her share of the related gains. (Every year, each shareholder's portion of the gains will be reported to her on Form 1099-DIV sent by the fund company.)

What makes the situation particularly odd is that, in any given year, the capital gains realized by the fund can vary (sometimes significantly) from the actual change in value of the shares of the fund.

EXAMPLE: Deborah buys a share of Mutual Fund XYZ on January 1 for $100. By the end of the year, the investments that the fund owns have (on average) decreased in value, and Deborah's share of the mutual fund is now worth $95.

However, during the course of the year, the mutual fund sold only one stock from the portfolio. That stock was sold for a short term capital gain. Deborah is going to be responsible for paying tax on her share of the capital gain, despite the fact that her share in the mutual fund has decreased in value.

Note how even in years when the value decreases, it's possible that the investors will be re-

41

sponsible for paying taxes on a gain. Of course, the opposite is also true. There can be years when the fund increases in value, but the stock sales made by the fund result in a capital loss. And thus the investors have an increase in the value of their holdings, but they don't have to pay any taxes for the time being.

Capital Gains from Selling Your Home

Selling a home that you've owned for many years can result in an absolutely enormous long term capital gain. Good news: It's very likely that you can exclude (that is, not pay tax on) a large portion—or even all—of that gain.

If you meet three requirements, you're allowed to exclude up to $250,000 of gain ($500,000 for married couples filing jointly). The three requirements are as follows:

1. For the two years prior to the date of sale, you did not exclude gain from the sale of another home.
2. During the five years prior to the date of sale, you owned the home for at least two years.
3. During the five years prior to the date of sale, you lived in the home as your main home for at least two years.

42

Note: To meet the second and third requirements, the two-year time periods do not necessarily have to be made up of 24 consecutive months.

EXAMPLE: Jason purchased a home on January 1, 2006. He lived there until May 1, 2007 (16 months). He then moved to another city (without selling his original home) and lived there until January 1, 2008. On January 1, 2008 Jason moved back into his original home and lived there until September 1, 2008 (8 months) when he sold the house for a $200,000 gain.

Jason can exclude the gain because he meets all three requirements. The fact that his 24 months using the home as his main home were not consecutive does not prevent him from excluding the gain.

Capital Losses

Of course, things don't always go exactly as planned. When you sell something for less than you paid for it, you incur what is known as a capital loss. Like capital gains, capital losses are characterized as either short term or long term, based upon whether the holding period of the asset was greater than or less than one year.

Each year, you add up all of your short term capital losses, and deduct them from your short term capital gains. Then you add up all of your long term

43

capital losses and deduct them from your long term capital gains. If the end result is a positive LTCG and a positive STCG, the LTCG will be taxed at a maximum rate of 15%, and the STCG will be taxed at ordinary income tax rates. If the end result is a net capital loss, you can deduct up to $3,000 of it from your ordinary income. The remainder of the capital loss can be carried forward to deduct in future years until it is eventually used in its entirety.

EXAMPLE 1: For 2008, Aaron has:
$5,000 in short term capital gains,
$3,000 in short term capital losses,
$4,000 in long term capital gains, and
$2,500 in long term capital losses.

For the year, Aaron will have a net STCG of $2,000 ($5,000-$3,000) and a net LTCG of $1,500 ($4,000-$2,500). His STCG will be taxed at his ordinary income tax rate, and his LTCG will be taxed at 15%.

EXAMPLE 2: For 2008, Seth has:
$2,000 in short term capital gains,
$3,500 in short term capital losses,
$3,000 in long term capital gains, and
$5,000 in long term capital losses.

Seth has a net short term capital loss of $1,500 and a net long term capital loss of $2,000. So his total capital loss is $3,500. For this capital loss, he can take a $3,000 deduction against his other income, and he can use the remaining $500 to offset his capital gains next year.

So what happens when you have a net gain in the short term category and a net loss in the long term category, or vice versa? In short, you net the two against each other, and the remaining gain or loss is taxed according to its character (that is, short term or long term).

EXAMPLE 1: For 2008, Kyle has:
$5,000 net short term capital gain and
$4,000 net long term capital loss.

Kyle will subtract his LTCL from his STCG, leaving him with a STCG of $1,000. This will be taxed according to his ordinary income tax bracket.

EXAMPLE 2: For 2008, Christopher has:
$3,000 net short term capital loss and
$6,000 net long term capital gain.

Christopher will subtract his STCL from his LTCG, leaving him with a LTCG of $3,000. This will be taxed at a maximum of 15%.

EXAMPLE 3: For 2008, Jeremy has:
$2,000 net short term capital gain and
$3,000 net long term capital loss.

Jeremy will subtract his LTCL from his STCG, leaving him with a $1,000 LTCL. Because this is below the $3,000 threshold, he can deduct the entire $1,000 loss from his ordinary income.

EXAMPLE 4: For 2008, Jessi has:
$2,000 net long term capital gain and
$4,000 net short term capital loss.

Jessi will subtract her STCL from her LTCG, leaving her with a $2,000 STCL. Because this is below the $3,000 threshold, she can deduct the entire $2,000 loss from her ordinary income.

Chapter 6 Simple Summary

- If an asset is held for one year or less, then sold for a gain, the Short Term Capital Gain will be taxed at ordinary income tax rates.

- If an asset is held for more than one year, then sold for a gain, the Long Term Capital Gain will be taxed at a maximum rate of 15%.

- If you have a net capital loss for the year, you can subtract up to $3,000 of that loss from your ordinary income. The remainder of the loss can be carried forward to offset income in future years.

- Mutual fund shareholders have to pay taxes each year as a result of the net gains incurred by the fund. This is unique in that taxes have to be paid before the asset is sold.

- If you sell your home for a gain, and you meet certain requirements (see page 42), you may be eligible to exclude up to $250,000 of the gain ($500,000 if married filing jointly).

PART THREE

Important Deductions and Credits

CHAPTER SEVEN

Alphabet Soup: IRAs and 401(k)s

You don't have to be a CPA to understand the benefit of taking advantage of every tax deduction you're entitled to. The even larger advantage, however, comes when you receive deductions for things that you'd be wise to do anyway. For example...

Investing via a Traditional IRA

IRAs are simply investment accounts with some additional benefits and restrictions tacked on. The main benefit of contributing money to an IRA is that when you do, you get an above the line deduction for the amount of the contribution. (For a review of above and below the line deductions see page 23.)

49

After money has been contributed to an IRA, you can invest it in (almost) anything you'd like: stocks, bonds, mutual funds, CDs, etc. The money then continues to grow tax-free while it remains in the account. However, when you do eventually take money out of the account, the amount of the withdrawal is taxable as income.

Because of this tax-deduction-now, taxable-withdrawals-later structure, IRAs are sometimes referred to as "tax-deferred" investment accounts. There are two primary advantages to tax-deferred investing.

The first advantage is the result of good timing. Assuming you make your contributions during your pre-retirement years, you get your deductions in years while your income is at a high point, thus maximizing the value of the deduction. Then, when you begin to make withdrawals during retirement, you'll be taxed on the withdrawal, but by then you'll likely be in a lower tax bracket because you're no longer working.

The second benefit to tax-deferred investing is that your money can grow more quickly when it's not being taxed on its growth along the way. Even when you account for the fact that it will be taxable when you withdraw it, you still (usually) come out with more after-tax money than you would if you were simply investing in a taxable investment account.

The Rules for Investing in an IRA

In exchange for granting you a tax deduction for investing in an IRA, the government requires you to jump through a few hoops in order to take full advantage of having an IRA. There are restrictions on both the deduction that you get for investing in your IRA and on your ability to withdraw money from your IRA.

First, as of 2009, annual IRA contributions are limited to the lesser of:

- $5,000 (unless you're 50 or older, in which case you're allowed to invest up to $6,000), or
- Your taxable compensation for the year.

Second, if your income reaches a certain level, (see below) you may no longer qualify to receive a deduction for the amount that you contribute to your IRA. However, even if you do reach this point, you are still allowed to make a contribution to an IRA, and you will not be taxed on the growth until you withdraw the money from the account.

The income limits for being able to receive a deduction for IRA contributions only come into play if either you or your spouse is covered by a retirement plan at work (such as a 401(k), which we'll discuss shortly).

If you are covered by a retirement plan at work, your deduction for an IRA contribution will begin to decrease (and eventually disappear entirely) as your Modified Adjusted Gross Income (MAGI)[1] for 2009 surpasses:

- $89,000 for married taxpayers filing jointly.
- $55,000 for single taxpayers.

If your spouse is covered by a retirement plan at work, but you are not, your deduction for an IRA contribution begins to be phased out once your joint Modified Adjusted Gross Income passes $166,000 for 2009.

Restrictions on IRA Withdrawals

Congress's goal when originally creating the laws that allow for IRAs was to encourage people to save for retirement, so they implemented some restrictions regarding when you're allowed to take money out of an IRA.

The most notable restriction is that any withdrawals (also referred to as "IRA distributions") that you make before age 59½ will be subject to a

---

[1] Your Adjusted Gross Income with a few specific deductions added back in. See Chapter 2 of IRS Publication 590 for more info: http://www.irs.gov/publications/p590/ch02.html

10% tax, in addition to being subject to normal income taxes.

There are several exceptions to the 59½ rule, however. A withdrawal will not be subject to the additional 10% tax if:

- You are disabled.
- You have unreimbursed medical expenses that are more than 7.5% of your adjusted gross income.
- The distributions are used to pay for qualified higher education expenses (e.g., college expenses for yourself, your spouse, your child, or grandchild).
- You use the distribution to buy or build your first home. (Note: only the first $10,000 of distributions for this purpose will be free from the additional 10% tax.)

Roth IRAs: Tax-Free Earnings

Our discussion of IRAs up to this point has related to the type of IRA known as a "Traditional IRA." In addition to Traditional IRAs, there is an alternative type of IRA known as a Roth IRA.

The biggest difference between a Traditional IRA and a Roth IRA is that you do *not* get a deduction for contributions to a Roth IRA. Instead, when you take money out of your Roth IRA, it will be tax

53

free. Even the earnings on your contributions come out free of tax.

Restrictions on Roth IRAs

However, as you'd expect, there are some rules that go along with investing via a Roth IRA. First, there are contribution limits. These are the same as for a Traditional IRA. That is, for 2009 you can contribute the lesser of:

- $5,000 ($6,000 if you're age 50 or over), or
- The total of your taxable compensation for the year.

Also, your eligibility to contribute to a Roth IRA is reduced (and eventually eliminated) as your income increases:

- For single taxpayers and taxpayers filing as head of household, the amount you can contribute to a Roth IRA begins to decrease as your Modified Adjusted Gross Income surpasses $105,000. Once your MAGI reaches $120,000, you can no longer contribute to a Roth IRA.
- For married taxpayers filing jointly, the amount you can contribute to a Roth IRA begins to decrease as your Modified Adjusted

54

Gross Income surpasses $166,000. Once your MAGI reaches $176,000, you can no longer contribute to a Roth IRA.

Note that the income limits are much higher for Roth IRAs than they are for Traditional IRAs.

Distributions from Roth IRAs are subject to a 10% additional tax unless they meet certain requirements (almost identical to the requirements for Traditional IRA distributions). The biggest difference is that in addition to the other requirements, the distribution must be made at least 5 years after the first contribution was made to your Roth IRA.

Which Type of IRA is Better for Me?

The conventional wisdom when it comes to choosing between a Traditional IRA and a Roth IRA is that it comes down to your current income level, and how you expect that to compare to your income level during retirement.

EXAMPLE 1: Pam works as an upper-level manager at a graphic design firm. Her employer does not currently offer a retirement plan. She is unmarried and earns $100,000 annually.

Given the high probability that Pam will be in a lower tax bracket once she retires than she is in at the moment, it makes sense for her to contribute to a traditional IRA. The value of receiving a deduction now, while she's in the 28% tax bracket, likely outweighs the value of being able to make tax-free withdrawals once she's retired.

EXAMPLE 2: Laurie is a college student who recently got a raise at her summer job. She's going to earn approximately $5,000 this summer. Laurie doesn't work during the school year.

A Roth IRA is almost certainly the best option for Laurie. At the moment, she's only in the 10% tax bracket, so the value of a deduction from an IRA contribution isn't that great. The ability to grow her money (and eventually withdraw it) free of tax in a Roth IRA is much more valuable.

EXAMPLE 3: Carlos is currently unmarried, and he earns $80,000 per year. His employer offers a 401(k) plan to which he can contribute. After making the maximum contribution to his 401(k) (discussed in the next section), Carlos still wants to invest more money for retirement.

Despite the fact that a contribution to a Traditional IRA would be appealing, he has no option here. Because he has a retirement plan at work, and because of his income level, he is ineligible for a deduction for a Traditional IRA contribution. If he wants to contribute to an IRA, he must use a Roth IRA.

If Carlos made, for example, $200,000 annually, he would be unable to contribute to either type of IRA because his income would exceed the limits for both Traditional IRAs and Roth IRAs.

401(k) Plans

A 401(k) plan—named after Section 401(k) of the tax code—is a deferred compensation plan through which an employee can choose to have some of her wages/salary deposited into a tax-deferred investment account. In other words, having a 401(k) is very much like having an IRA through your work. There are, however, several noteworthy differences between 401(k) accounts and IRAs.

Investing via a 401(k) Account

The first and foremost difference is that 401(k) accounts have much higher contribution limits than IRAs. If you are under age 50, your maximum contribution limit is $16,500 for 2009. If you are 50 or over, your contribution limit for 2009 is $22,000.

A second, potentially important, difference is that in a 401(k) your investment options will be limited to a pre-selected group of mutual funds. This isn't necessarily going to be a problem, as you're likely to find several suitable investment choices

57

within the pre-selected list. However, if there is a particular mutual fund company that you want to use, you might be out of luck.

401(k) Distributions

Like IRA distributions, distributions from a 401(k) will be subject to an additional 10% tax if you are under age 59½. However, the list of exceptions to the 59½ rule is different with 401(k) accounts than it is with IRAs. The most important differences are that:

- Distributions for a first time home purchase *will* be subject to the 10% additional tax.
- Distributions for paying higher education expenses *will* be subject to the 10% additional tax.
- Distributions made to an employee after separation from service—if the separation occurred during or after the calendar year in which the employee reached age 55—will *not* be subject to the additional 10% tax.

401(k) Rollovers

When you leave your job, you can transfer your 401(k) into either a Traditional IRA or a 401(k) with

58

your new employer. This nontaxable transfer is known as a 401(k) rollover. Generally, a rollover is a wise idea, because it will allow you a broader range of investment options and will allow you to escape from the administrative fees charged by most 401(k) plans.

Any financial planner should be able to help you with rolling over a 401(k). Be careful, however, to avoid paying excessive mutual fund commissions when you rollover your 401(k). Many advisors will try to persuade you to invest your newly-rolled-over IRA in mutual funds that charge very high commissions, when the funds are in fact no better than low cost, commission-free index funds. If you meet with an advisor who does this, thank him for his time, and start (or continue) searching for another advisor.

Chapter 7 Simple Summary

- Traditional IRAs allow you to get an above the line deduction for saving for your retirement. However, there are restrictions to who can get a deduction for contributing to a traditional IRA (see page 51).

- Roth IRAs allow you to invest for retirement without being taxed upon the interest or growth of your investments. Again, there are restrictions as to who can contribute to a Roth IRA (see page 54).

- For the most part, if you withdraw money from your IRA prior to turning $59\frac{1}{2}$, the withdrawal will be subject to an extra 10% tax. (See page 53 for types of early withdrawals that are *not* subject to the additional tax.)

- Investing in a 401(k) at work is much like investing in an IRA. The biggest difference is that the contribution limit is much higher ($16,500 for 2009).

- 401(k) distributions taken prior to age $59\frac{1}{2}$ are generally subject to an extra 10% tax. As with IRAs, there are some exceptions (see page 58).

CHAPTER EIGHT

Other Important Deductions

Rather than try and discuss every obscure deduction that exists (a nearly impossible feat), we'll cover a handful of deductions that you'll very likely be able to use at some point.

Home Mortgage Interest

In most cases, if you own a home, you can deduct (as an itemized/below the line deduction[1]) any interest that you pay on your mortgage. As you'd expect, there are several requirements that must be met in order to take the deduction.

---

[1] As a reminder, see page 23 for a discussion of above the line vs. below the line deductions.

61

First, the mortgage must be "secured debt." All this means is that your home must be used as collateral for the loan. Of course, most homeowners' mortgages meet this requirement.

Next, the proceeds from the mortgage must have been used to purchase, build, or improve your home (or second home). In order to deduct mortgage interest paid on a second home, you must either:

- Not rent the home out to anyone else, or
- Live in the home for (at least) the greater of 14 days or 10% of the number of days that the home is rented out at fair rental value.

EXAMPLE: Dan owns two homes. He rents the second one out for 200 days during 2009. Over the course of the year, he lives in the home for a period of two weeks. Dan cannot deduct mortgage interest paid on his second home because he did not live in it for at least 10% of the number of days it was rented out.

Finally, if your mortgage balances were greater than $1,000,000 at any point in the year, it's possible that you might not be able to deduct all of the mortgage interest paid over the course of the year.[1]

---

[1] For more information about this limitation—or about the home mortgage interest deduction in general—see IRS Publication 936 available at http://www.irs.gov/publications/p936/

Charitable Contributions

As you probably know if you've ever been solicited for a donation, you're entitled to an itemized deduction for contributions that you make to charitable organizations. As you'd expect, there are some restrictions.

For example, if you make a contribution from which you'll also receive some benefit, you're only allowed to take a deduction for the amount by which the contribution exceeds the fair market value of the benefit that you receive.

EXAMPLE: Steve pays $100 for a ticket to a fundraiser dinner at his church. The value of the dinner provided is approximately $20. Steve can only deduct $80 for the contribution ($100 ticket minus $20 benefit received).

Donating Property

Generally, when you donate property to a qualified organization, you're entitled to a deduction equal to the fair market value of the property.

However, if you are donating property that would trigger a short-term capital gain (or ordinary income) if you sold it, your deduction is limited to the fair market value of the property, minus the property's increase in value.

63

EXAMPLE: Liliana owns shares of Apple® that she purchased 18 months ago for a total of $400. The shares are currently worth $600. If she donates them to a qualified organization, she's entitled to a deduction for their fair market value ($600).

If, however, she had only owned the shares for 6 months (such that a sale of them would cause a short-term capital gain), she would only be entitled to a $400 deduction. ($600 fair market value minus the $200 of appreciation.)

Donating Services

Services donated to qualified organizations are *not* deductible. However, if you incur any expenses in the course of providing your donated services, you may claim a deduction for those expenses.

EXAMPLE: Barrie is a freelance web designer. He decides to donate his services to a local church, creating a website for them for which he would ordinarily charge $500. In order to create the website, he spends $40 on a template for his web design software. Barrie cannot deduct the value of his services, but he can deduct the $40 spent on the template.

Recordkeeping for Charitable Contributions

For cash contributions[1] of under $250, all you're required to keep as proof is a canceled check or a credit card statement indicating the amount and date of the contribution as well as the name of the organization.

For cash contributions of $250 or more, you will need to get some form of written acknowledgement of the contribution from the organization to which you made the donation. The acknowledgement must:

- State the amount of cash you donated,
- State the date of the donation, and
- State an estimate of the value (if any) of any goods or services that you received in exchange for the contribution.

For noncash contributions of less than $250, you'll need to keep a receipt or record indicating:

- the name of the organization,
- the date and location of the contribution, and
- a "reasonably detailed" description of the property contributed.

---

[1] In this instance, "cash contributions" refers to contributions made by cash, check, or credit/debit card.

65

For noncash contributions between $250 and $500, you will need the same records as for contributions below $250, plus an acknowledgement of the donation from the recipient organization. As with cash contributions, the acknowledgement must state the value (if any) of any goods or services that you received in exchange for your donation.

For noncash contributions between $500 and $5,000, you will need the same records as for contributions between $250 and $500. You will also need to keep records of the following information:

- How you originally obtained the property (purchase, gift, etc.),
- The approximate date that you obtained the property, and
- Your adjusted cost basis in the property. (See page 38 for a review of adjusted cost basis.)

Noncash contributions of greater than $5,000 require all of the same records, plus a written appraisal of the property, provided by a qualified appraiser.

Limit on Charitable Contribution Deductions

One final point of note about deductions for charitable contributions is that there's a limitation to the

66

maximum deduction you are allowed. What the limit is depends upon what type of organizations you're contributing to, as well as what type of property you're contributing.

Luckily, these limitations don't affect most taxpayers, as they don't kick in until your charitable contributions exceed 20% of your Adjusted Gross Income.[1]

Deduction for Medical Expenses

A deduction is allowed for unreimbursed medical expenses. However, most taxpayers do not get to use this deduction as a result of two factors. First, it's an itemized deduction. And, more importantly, the amount of the deduction is reduced by 7.5% of your Adjusted Gross Income. In other words, the deduction is only helpful if (and to the extent that) your medical expenses exceed 7.5% of your AGI.

When calculating your deduction for medical expenses, you can include medical and dental expenses paid for yourself, your spouse, and your dependents. Deductible expenses include payments made for the cure, prevention, diagnosis, mitigation, or treatment of disease. With the exception of insulin, only prescription drugs can be included in the deduction.

---

[1] For more information about these limitations, see IRS Publication 526, available at http://www.irs.gov/publications/p526/

67

Chapter 8 Simple Summary

- If you own a home, you are most likely entitled to an itemized deduction for interest that you pay on your secured mortgage.

- If your mortgage balance exceeds $1,000,000, it's possible that some (or all) of the interest may be nondeductible.

- Donations of cash or property to charitable organizations can be taken as itemized deductions. Donated services, however, are not deductible.

- Be sure to keep excellent records of any charitable contributions that you make.

- An itemized deduction is allowed for medical expenses to the extent that they exceed 7.5% of your Adjusted Gross Income.

CHAPTER NINE

Important Credits

As with deductions, rather than attempt to cover every possible credit, let's just take a look at those that are most commonly available. Remember, credits are especially valuable in that they reduce your tax dollar for dollar, as opposed to deductions, which reduce your taxable income. That is, a credit of a given amount is worth more to you than a deduction of the same amount.

Earned Income Credit

If in 2009 you work and you earn less than $48,279, you may be eligible for a credit known as the Earned Income Credit. The Earned Income Credit is a tax break for people whom Congress has determined to be lower-income taxpayers.

In order to be able to claim the credit, you must meet one of the following requirements:

- You have three or more qualifying children and you earn less than $43,279 ($48,279 if married filing jointly),
- You have two qualifying children and you earn less than $40,295 ($45,295 if married filing jointly),
- You have one qualifying child and you earn less than $35,463 ($40,463 if married filing jointly), or
- You do not have a qualifying child and you earn less than $13,440 ($18,440 if married filing jointly).

You aren't responsible for calculating the amount of the credit, as the IRS will do it for you. If, however, you want to know ahead of time how much your credit will be, check the table in the appendix of IRS Publication 596.[1] You'll see that the credit varies as a function of both:

- The number of qualifying children you have, and
- The lower of your Earned Income or Adjusted Gross Income.

---

[1] Available at http://www.irs.gov/publications/p596/apa.html

Retirement Savings Contribution Credit

The Retirement Savings Contribution Credit is a credit available to you if you contributed to either an IRA (of any kind) or a retirement plan at work, such as a 401(k). To claim this credit, your Adjusted Gross Income for 2009 must be less than:

- $55,500 if married filing jointly,
- $41,625 if filing as head of household, or
- $27,750 if single or married filing separately.

The amount of the credit can be anywhere from 10%-50% of the contributions you made to your retirement plans. If you're at the lower end of the income spectrum, it will be nearer to 50%, and it will be nearer to 10% if you're earning an amount that would almost make you ineligible. Form 8880[1] has a table showing what percentage to use for calculating your credit.

EXAMPLE: Lee is single, and he earns $26,000 over the course of 2009. During the year he contributes $1,500 to a Roth IRA. Form 8880 shows that at $26,000, a person's credit is equal to 10% of his retirement account contributions. Therefore, Lee's

---

[1] Available at www.irs.gov/pub/irs-pdf/f8880.pdf

71

Retirement Savings Contribution Credit will be $150 for 2009.

What makes the Retirement Savings Contribution Credit so wonderful is the fact that it rewards you for doing something that is beneficial to do anyway. If you qualify for the credit, you're essentially getting (at least) an extra 10% return on your money, in addition to whatever it earns on its own.

Child and Dependent Care Credit

If, during the course of the year, you pay somebody to care for your child (or other dependent) so that you (and your spouse, if you're married) can work, you're likely eligible for the Child and Dependent Care Credit. In order to claim the credit you must:

- Have earned income during the year. (If you're married, your spouse must also have earned income.)
- Pay child care or dependent care expenses so that you (and your spouse, if married) can work or look for work.
- Make the payments to somebody who cannot be claimed as your dependent. (For example, paying your 14-year-old son to watch your 8-year-old daughter doesn't count.)
- Identify the care provider on your tax return.

- File a joint return with your spouse if you're married.

Also, the payments cannot be made to the parent of the child for whom the care is being provided.

The amount of the credit is a percentage of the expenses paid. The percentage varies as a function of your income (the more you make, the lower the percentage) and can be found in IRS Publication 503.[1]

The amount of expenses that you use to calculate the credit is limited in two ways. First, it's limited to your earned income during the course of the year. (If you're married, it's limited to the lesser of your earned income or your spouse's earned income.) Second, it's limited to $3,000 for one child or dependent, or $6,000 for two more or children/dependents.

First-Time Homebuyer Credit

As a result of the American Recovery and Reinvestment Act of 2009, there is a credit available to homebuyers who purchased their first home between January 1, 2009 and December 1, 2009. The credit is calculated as 10% of the home purchase price, limited to $8,000.

---

[1] Available at http://www.irs.gov/publications/p503/

73

It's important to note that if the home in question ceases to be the taxpayer's main residence within three years of the date of purchase, the credit will have to be paid back to the Federal government.

Chapter 9 Simple Summary

- If you worked during 2009, and your earned income is less than $48,279, it's possible that you're eligible for the Earned Income Credit. See page 70 for specific requirements.

- If you contributed to an IRA or a retirement plan at work, and your 2009 income is below $27,750 ($55,500 if married filing jointly), you're probably eligible for the Retirement Savings Contribution Credit.

- If you pay somebody to care for your child or other dependent so that you (and your spouse, if you're married) can work or look for work, you're likely eligible for the Child and Dependent Care Credit.

- Taxpayers who purchase their first home between January 1, 2009 and December 1, 2009 are eligible for a credit of 10% of the home's purchase price, up to $8,000.

CHAPTER TEN

Deductions & Credits for Education Expenses

Given that the tax law is (usually) set up to reward things that Congress has decided are beneficial to our country, it's no surprise that there are tax breaks available for people paying for higher education expenses.

Tuition and Fees Deduction

If you pay higher education expenses for yourself, your spouse, or your dependent, you may be entitled to the tuition and fees deduction of up to $4,000. In order to qualify for the deduction (an above-the-line deduction), you must:

- Have a Modified Adjusted Gross Income of less than $80,000 ($160,000 if married filing jointly).
- Not be able to be claimed as a dependent on somebody else's return.
- Not be married filing separately.

Qualifying Education Expenses

In order to be deductible, the expenses must be paid to a university, college, vocational school, or other postsecondary educational institution. Deductible expenses include tuition, fees, and other course-related expenses that are required to be paid to the institution as a condition for enrollment (or attendance).

EXAMPLE: Jack is attending school to be a filmmaker. In addition to his tuition, he's required to pay $500 per semester for use of the school's film studio. Because he is required to pay the $500 to the school in order to attend classes, the expense can be included as a qualifying education expense.

EXAMPLE: Lee is attending school for a degree in Spanish. Each semester, he is required to buy several textbooks and DVDs to use for his courses. However, because his school doesn't require that he buy the materials from the school—he could buy them online

76

on Amazon®, for instance—the cost does not count as a qualifying education expense.

Two more points of note about the tuition and fees deduction:

1. Under no circumstances does room and board count as a qualifying education expense.
2. It doesn't matter whether or not the money used to pay the expenses was obtained with a loan.

Education Credits

As an alternative to taking the tuition and fees deduction for higher education expenses, you may be able to use one of two credits: The Lifetime Learning Credit or the Hope Credit.

Each year, for a given student, you can only use one of the three (the deduction, or one of the two credits). As such, this area is one in which it's particularly valuable to know your options so that you can make the best decision.[1]

---

[1] There is an excellent chart comparing the three options in the appendix to IRS Publication 970 available at: http://www.irs.gov/publications/p970/ar02.html

77

As with the tuition and fees deduction, you can only claim a credit for higher education expenses paid for yourself, your spouse, or a dependent.

Hope Credit

The Hope Credit (sometimes referred to as the American Opportunity Tax Credit) is available for students who are in their first four years of postsecondary education and who are enrolled at least "half-time." The amount of the credit is the sum of the first $2,000 of qualified education expenses paid for the student, plus 25% of the next $2,000 of qualified expenses. (Note that this means that the maximum credit per student is $2,500 for 2009.)

Your eligibility to claim the Hope Credit begins to decrease as your Modified Adjusted Gross Income exceeds $80,000 for 2009 ($160,000 if married filing jointly). Once your MAGI reaches $90,000 ($180,000 if married filing jointly), you'll no longer be eligible to use the credit.

In addition to the expenses that can be used when calculating the tuition and fees deduction, expenditures for "course materials" can be used for purposes of calculating the Hope Credit. "Course materials" includes books and supplies needed for a course, whether or not the materials are purchased from the educational institution as a condition of enrollment or attendance.

Lifetime Learning Credit

The Lifetime Learning Credit is available for any student enrolled in postsecondary education or any employee enrolled in courses to acquire or improve job skills. The amount of the credit is 20% of the first $10,000 of qualified education expenses. (Note that this means that the maximum credit per student is $2,000 for 2009.)

As with the tuition and fees deduction, the only expenses that can be considered when calculating the Lifetime Learning Credit are:

- Tuition and fees
- Other course-related expenses that are required to be paid to the institution as a condition for enrollment or attendance.

Your eligibility to claim the Lifetime Learning Credit begins to decrease as your Modified Adjusted Gross Income exceeds $50,000 for 2009 ($100,000 if married filing jointly). Once your MAGI reaches $60,000 ($120,000 if married filing jointly), you'll no longer be eligible to use the credit.

Unlike the Hope Credit, there is no limit to the number of years that the Lifetime Learning Credit can be used for a given student. However, the Lifetime Learning Credit can only be claimed for one student per tax return per year.

EXAMPLE: Katie and Alex are siblings. Alex is a freshman in college, and Katie is a senior (in her fifth year of college). With the help of some student loans, their family spends $10,000 for tuition for each of them for the year.

The family should probably claim the Hope Credit for Alex, because it will allow for a credit of $2,500, as opposed to the $2,000 that would be allowed via the Lifetime Learning Credit. Also, by *not* using the Lifetime Learning Credit for Alex, the family can still use the Lifetime Learning Credit for Katie. (Katie is ineligible for the Hope Credit, because she is in her fifth year of college.) In total, the family will be able to claim $4,500-worth of education-related credits.

Chapter 10 Simple Summary

- If you pay higher education expenses for yourself, your spouse, or a dependent, you can likely deduct up to $4,000 of those expenses per year.

- Students in their first four years of postsecondary education may be eligible to claim the Hope Credit (of up to $2,500 for 2009).

- Students enrolled in postsecondary education may be eligible for the Lifetime Learning Credit (which can be as large as $2,000 in 2009). Only one Lifetime Learning Credit can be claimed per tax return per year.

- For a given student's expenses, you can only use one of: the Hope Credit, the Lifetime Learning Credit, or the tuition and fees deduction.

PART FOUR

Other Important Things to Know

CHAPTER ELEVEN

Tax Forms

One of the more intimidating aspects of taxation in the United States is the seemingly endless list of tax forms. There are Forms 1040, 8889, 2106, 8880, and countless more, not to mention Schedules A, B, C, D, and so on.

What makes matters worse is that even looking at all the tiny print and numerous boxes to be filled-in on just one form can be enough to make an uninitiated taxpayer dizzy.

The good news is that the situation is really far less complicated than it appears. For example, most likely, you'll only have to fill out a handful of forms for your annual tax return (Form 1040, and a couple accompanying schedules or forms). Many people don't even have it that bad: Every year, thousands of taxpayers are eligible to file Form 1040-EZ (which takes only a few minutes to prepare) and be done with the whole thing.

What further simplifies the situation is that each of the forms comes with a set of line-by-line instructions that is fairly easy to understand. When done carefully and one step at a time, even the more difficult tax forms can be prepared successfully by somebody with only a very basic understanding of taxation.

Form 1040

Form 1040[1] is the primary form for an individual's income tax return. In other words, it's the one single form that you're going to be filing every year, almost regardless of circumstances. As a result, it makes sense to take a little time to become familiar with it.

Form 1040 is only two pages long, and the first quarter of the form is simply filling in information like your name, address, filing status, etc. After filling out your personal information, you calculate how many exemptions you can take. (As we discussed in Chapter 2, it's one for you, one for your spouse, and one for each of your dependents.)

In the next section you essentially list each of your different sources (and amounts) of income: wages, interest, dividends, business income, etc. You then add up all of your income sources to arrive at your "Total Income."

---

[1] Available at http://www.irs.gov/pub/irs-pdf/f1040.pdf.

The next section is where you enter all of your above the line deductions (such as traditional IRA contributions). You then subtract the total of your above the line deductions from your Total Income to arrive at your Adjusted Gross Income. Next, you subtract either your standard deduction or the sum of your itemized deductions to arrive at your Taxable Income.

Finally, you use your Taxable Income to determine your total income tax. From this number, subtract any credits for which you're eligible, and then compare the remainder to the amount that was withheld from your paychecks over the course of the year for Federal income taxes. This will show whether you have a refund coming or if it's time to write a check to the United States Treasury.

As you can see, the flow of the form is very logical, with everything happening in the order that you would expect.

Form 1040-EZ

If you meet a handful of requirements, you'll be allowed to file Form 1040-EZ instead of a regular Form 1040. Form 1040-EZ is exactly what it sounds like: An easier version of Form 1040. (The 2008 version is only thirteen lines long.) To be eligible to file Form 1040-EZ you must:

- Be either single or married filing jointly.
- Be under age 65 at the end of the tax year. (The same goes for your spouse.)
- Not claim any dependents.
- Have a taxable income of less than $100,000.
- Not claim any credits aside from the Earned Income Credit.
- Have earned only the following types of income: wages, salaries, tips, unemployment compensation, or less than $1,500 of interest.

Schedules for Form 1040

In the field of taxation, a Schedule is an attachment to a Form. Most schedules that you'll hear about are attachments to your Form 1040. The most frequently used schedules include:

Schedule A: If you plan to itemize, this schedule is where you will list and sum all of your itemized deductions.

Schedule B: This schedule is used to report interest and dividend income. Generally, you won't be required to fill it out unless you've had over $1,500 of interest or dividends.

Schedule C: If you run a business as a sole proprietor, you will use this schedule to calculate and report your business's profit or loss.

Schedule D: Used to report capital gains and losses.

Schedule E: Used to report income (or loss) from rental real estate, royalties, partnerships, S-Corporations, estates, or trusts.

How to Know What Form(s) and Schedules to Use

You won't have any trouble with determining what forms or schedules you have to fill out. Simply proceed line-by-line through your Form 1040, and when you need to fill out an additional form or schedule, it will usually be stated right on your 1040.

For example, if you have income from a business, you'll see that right on Form 1040, Line 12 (Business Income or Loss) you are asked to attach Schedule C or C-EZ.

Chapter 11 Simple Summary

- Form 1040 is the primary form you'll be filling out every year. If, however, you meet the requirements on page 86, you can file Form 1040-EZ.

- Don't worry about memorizing what form or schedule to use for what. When you need to fill out an extra form or schedule, it will generally say so right on your Form 1040.

CHAPTER TWELVE

State Income Taxes

It's likely that, in addition to Federal income taxes, you're responsible for paying income tax to your state as well. While income tax rates vary from state to state, the general premise is the same (with, of course, the exception of the handful of states that have no income tax).

How it Works in Most States

Most state income tax returns are short and easy to prepare. Rather than making you go through another calculation to determine your taxable income, they simply allow you to enter your taxable income from your Federal Form 1040.

Your taxable income from your Federal return is then usually subjected to a few adjustments—if,

89

for example, your state doesn't allow deductions for certain expenses that are deductible for Federal purposes. After making these adjustments, you can generally calculate your state income tax for the year by looking up your taxable income in a table that's provided in the form's instructions.

For the most part, the only time a state return becomes complicated is when you live (and work) in multiple states over the course of a year. And even then, it's not so bad. You simply have a little more paperwork to do, as each state will require you to fill out an extra form to calculate how much of your income was earned while working in that state as opposed to other states.

Where to Look for Information

One thing that can make state taxation somewhat more challenging is the fact that information about the topic is generally less accessible. When compared to the excellent usability of the IRS's website, many states' websites leave a great deal to be desired, and it frequently takes a little more work than you'd expect to find the answers to questions.

When it comes to state tax forms and their instructions, however, you shouldn't have any problem. Most forms are easy to find online. If you can't find them there, they're usually available around tax season at your local post offices and public libraries.

Deduction for State Income Taxes

If you plan on itemizing your deductions, you'll be happy to learn that you're allowed an itemized deduction (on your Federal return) for state and local income taxes paid over the course of the year. For 2009 the deduction would include:

- State and local income taxes withheld from your salary over the course of the year.
- State and local income taxes paid during 2009 for a prior year. (If, for example, you had to include a check with your 2008 state income tax return.)
- State and local estimated tax payments that you made during 2009.

The deduction for state and local income taxes does not, however, include penalties or interest paid along with those taxes.

EXAMPLE: Melissa files her 2008 state tax return on June 10th of 2009, making it approximately two months late. She has to send a check for $320, $100 of which was for interest and penalties for late filing.

For 2009, Melissa will be able to take an itemized deduction for the $220 in tax that she paid with her 2008 return (in addition to any state and local income taxes that are withheld from her paychecks over the course of the 2009). But she will not be able to deduct the $100 she paid for interest and penalties.

Chapter 12 Simple Summary

- Most states charge income taxes based upon a slightly-adjusted version of your taxable income from your Federal return. As such, preparing your state tax return will be easy after having prepared your Federal return.

- The best place to look for state tax information is online. If, however, you find that the Department of Revenue (or other corresponding agency) in your state has a mediocre website, you might want to try looking for resources locally—at a library, for instance—especially if all you need is a particular form and its instructions.

- Each year, you're allowed an itemized deduction on your Federal return for any state and local income taxes that you pay over the course of the year.

CHAPTER THIRTEEN

The Alternative Minimum Tax (AMT)

The Alternative Minimum Tax was created by the Tax Reform Act of 1969. The goal was to create a tax that would target a group of very high-income taxpayers who had managed to take advantage of so many tax benefits that they were paying little or no income tax despite their high income.

The AMT was later expanded by the Tax Reform Act of 1986 to capture a greater percentage of high-income taxpayers.

The Purpose of the AMT

The basic idea of the Alternative Minimum Tax was simple: Start with your gross income, subtract an exemption—one that would be sufficiently large to

93

rule out lower and middle income taxpayers—and subject the remaining income to a 26% tax. This tax (the "Alternative Minimum Tax") would then be compared to your income tax as calculated by the normal method. Whichever tax was higher was what you would be required to pay.

In essence, the AMT was designed to create a parallel tax system, one in which all deductions were replaced with one (very large) exemption. If your deductions under the normal system were greater than the amount of the exemption under this new system, you would end up having to pay tax under this new system. In effect, this would put a cap on how many deductions you could possibly take.

Not Just for the Super-Affluent Anymore

In recent years, the AMT has become rather controversial as a result of the fact that it no longer affects only high income taxpayers. The reason is that the exemption amount—the one that was supposed to be big enough to make it so that lower and middle income taxpayers wouldn't have to worry about the AMT—was not indexed for inflation.

Instead, the exemption amount has been adjusted on a year-by-year basis using short-term legislative "patches." As of this writing, the AMT exemption amount stands at $46,700 ($70,950 if married filing jointly). As a result, anybody earning over $46,700 could potentially be subject to the Alternative Minimum Tax. Given that the median household income in the United States is over $50,000[1], it's obvious that the AMT is no longer targeting only the highest earners.

The Big Problems with the AMT

The real issue isn't just that the AMT is affecting a rapidly growing number of taxpayers. Here in the United States, we're used to being taxed. We don't exactly enjoy it, but we at least expect it. We *know* that we have to pay income taxes.

The big problems with the AMT arise as a result of two factors:

1. Most taxpayers who owe AMT aren't even aware of the fact until they're contacted by the IRS.[2]
2. The actual calculation of the AMT is so complicated that many taxpayers have no option but to hire a professional to do it for them.

---

[1] $50,233 in 2007, according to the U.S. Census Bureau
[2] According to the National Taxpayer Advocate, a division of the IRS.

Of course, it's rather difficult to budget for the payment of a tax that you aren't even aware of. This unknown factor puts an unnecessary hardship on taxpayers.

Similarly, once your return is sufficiently complicated that you can no longer prepare it on your own, your tax burden is—essentially—increased. And this increased burden doesn't even go toward the things that taxes are supposed to pay for. It simply ends up in the pocket of a tax preparer. In the end, the AMT is a remarkably inefficient revenue generator for the Federal government.

Why Calculating AMT is So Difficult

Given that the basic idea behind the AMT is so simple (income, minus a big exemption, times 26% tax), you'd think that it wouldn't be too hard to calculate. Unfortunately, the actual calculation of the AMT doesn't mirror the simplicity of its conceptual basis in any way.

Instead, to calculate the AMT (using Form 6251), you must work backwards. You *start* with your taxable income from your Form 1040. From there you *add back* several "preference items," which consist of various deductions that you were allowed on your regular return, but aren't allowed for AMT purposes. The resulting answer is your Alternative Minimum Taxable Income.

From here, at least, the calculation is fairly easy. You subtract the AMT exemption (discussed on pages 94-95), and multiply the answer by either 26% or 28%, depending upon how high it is. This amount (your "tentative minimum tax") is compared to your regular income tax, and you are required to pay the greater of the two.

Chapter 13 Simple Summary

- The Alternative Minimum Tax was created as a sort of "catch-all" to prevent high income taxpayers from being able to take advantage of legal loopholes to escape paying income tax.

- Unfortunately, because the AMT exemption is not set to increase with inflation, the AMT now affects many middle class taxpayers, who were not the original target of the AMT.

- If you're subject to the AMT, be prepared to either hire a professional, or plan on spending plenty of time working on calculating it on your tax return.

- Calculating your Alternative Minimum Taxable Income involves working backwards from your taxable income, adding back several "preference" items, and subtracting a large exemption. Your AMT is then determined based upon the result of these calculations.

CONCLUSION

Do It Yourself Or
Find a Tax Professional?

An important question you'll have to answer each year is whether you plan to do your tax preparation yourself or find a professional to take care of it for you. As you can imagine, several factors should be considered.

In my opinion, however, one factor really trumps the rest: Do you even *want* to do it on your own? If preparing your own tax return sounds like a terrible experience to you, in all honesty, you're probably right. Also, if you're just trying to rush through it, you're more likely to make a mistake or miss a deduction that you could have taken.

If, on the other hand, you think you're the type who might find this sort of thing enjoyable, go ahead and give it a try. It's bound to be an educational experience, as it's practically impossible to prepare your own tax return without learning something in the process. Using software such as TurboTax® is obviously very popular (and understandably so), though you will definitely learn more by preparing your return by hand.

Furthermore, if you attempt to do it on your own, and decide that you're just not cut out for it, that's fine. You won't have any trouble finding a tax professional to finish off an already-started return. Similarly, if you prepare your own return but aren't completely confident in your abilities, it's absolutely reasonable to take it in to a professional and pay a small fee to get the return checked over to see if you missed anything.

But even if you do prepare your own return, don't write off the idea of finding a competent tax professional. Where a high quality tax professional really shows his/her worth isn't with tax preparation. The biggest advantage gained by having a tax advisor is that she'll often be able to find something that you could be doing differently in order to save yourself some money. And, frequently, these are things that you probably wouldn't catch just by doing your own tax return.

In summary, if you want to prepare your own return this year—or every year—go right ahead. You'll likely learn a lot, and you'll certainly save yourself some money on accounting fees. It would still be wise, however, to develop a working relationship with a tax advisor who you can trust with more complicated situations.

APPENDIX

<u>Helpful Online Resources</u>

<u>www.irs.gov</u>
  The IRS's website. Has an abundance of (surprisingly) easy to find information.

<u>www.simplesubjects.com/tax</u>
  Simple Subjects' tax website. Includes a wide variety of tax articles.

<u>www.taxalmanac.org</u>
  An excellent compendium of tax research resources, including a wonderful discussion board.

<u>IRS Publications</u>

Publication 503 – Child and Dependent Care Expenses

Publication 550 – Investment Income and Expenses

Publication 596 – Earned Income Credit

Taxes Made Simple: Income Taxes Explained in 100 Pages or Less

Publication 526 – Charitable Contributions

Publication 970 – Tax Benefits for Education

Publication 950 – Introduction to Estate and Gift Taxes

Publication 502 – Medical and Dental Expenses

Recommended Reading

How a Second Grader Beats Wall Street: Golden Rules Any Investor Can Learn, by Allan Roth

Oblivious Investing: Building Wealth by Ignoring the Noise, by Mike Piper

A Random Walk Down Wall Street: The Time-Tested Strategy for Successful Investing, by Burton Malkiel

Start Late, Finish Rich: A No-Fail Plan for Achieving Financial Freedom at Any Age, by David Bach

Surprisingly Simple: LLC vs. S-Corp vs. C-Corp Explained in 100 Pages or Less, by Mike Piper

INDEX